Mother

A Human Love Story

Matt Hopwood

BIRLINN

First published in 2019 by
Birlinn Limited
West Newington House
10 Newington Road
Edinburgh
EH9 1QS

www.birlinn.co.uk

ISBN 978 1 78027 512 3

British Library
Cataloguing-in-Publication Data
A catalogue record for this book
is available from the British Library.

Typeset in Bembo by Mark Blackadder
Printed and bound by PNB Print, Latvia

For my mother,
my grandmothers.
For all those who nurture
and allow themselves to be nurtured.

Contents

Foreword

Matt Hopwood is an unusual man. He walks a lot, talks quite a bit and listens, more than most. His long-term project, A Human Love Story, has grown out of his desire to hear other people's life narratives, to offer them a place where they can be vulnerable and share the making and breaking of who they are.

What's amazing about that simple idea – to let other people speak about what is important in their lives – is how it has developed. Matt likes to walk, so, at first, he just asked the people he encountered on his walks to talk to him. A few years on he has covered thousands of miles on foot, talked to hundreds of people, and the Human Love Story project has grown so that now it leads him rather than the other way around. At some point, it seemed a good idea to record the interviews so that Matt and those who had spoken to him could hear them again. At another point, a publisher suggested turning the stories into a book.

What was happening was that Matt's project was growing up. His child – A Human Love Story – was telling him what it wanted to be.

Raising children is a long process of letting go: of holding that tiny, fragile, beloved being close to you, protecting it, teaching it how to exist in the world, and then standing aside as it makes its own choices and moves on. Your children will leave you, as they should, as they must. You watch, heart thumping, as they do. And as your child learns, you learn too.

So *Mother: A Human Love Story* came out of all this. Matt's baby evolved and developed. This book is a child, talking about its mother; and it's a mother, talking about her child. There are tales of loving mothers, brave mothers, mothers who failed. (All motherhood, like all life, contains failure.) Some of the stories include the physical act of giving birth – that revolutionary transformation. Some tell how life shifts when you have a child, how your priorities change, how your molecules rearrange. You are the same person. You are utterly different. Others tell of caring and standing up for children who aren't biologically your own; of being a mother within a violent relationship; of being a mother within a patriarchal society. There are stories about accepting that motherhood is not for you – at least, not in terms of giving birth. Or what happens if your child dies. How you continue still to be a mother after that.

I love these stories. Each is individual, completely personal; and yet each contains universal truths, tells us something enormous that we already know, somewhere inside. Matt – the mother of this project – has allowed his child to grow, and this lovely book is the result.

Miranda Sawyer

Introduction

Just days before the commissioning of this book, my grand-mother of 101 years passed on. I stood looking down on the beautifully small body that had contained her enormous spirit, which was at times warm and wise, waspish and direct. I held her cooling hand, kissed her still-warm brow and cried for the loss of her physical presence, her particular voice, her steady gaze. We opened the windows to let the day welcome her spirit. The birds sang as we placed flowers around her silent body. Her being encompassed a family of children, grandchildren and great-grandchildren. She was the rooted mother, the enduring femi-nine, the solar star round which our numerous lives orbited.

And, through the lens of that tender physical loss, I began to engage in an exploration of the role of Mother in our lives and communities. Who is Mother? How do our profound and essential experiences of Mother shape our behaviour, how we form connection with others, with ourselves and with the world?

I wanted to meet with individuals of all genders and orien-tations and offer them a space to be vulnerable, to be heard and to share something of their experiences of Mother. I wanted to move into a place of unknowing, and be receptive to alternative expressions of understanding, to feel, to abide in something more expansive. As a white, middle-class, southern man from England I was becoming acutely aware of the limitations of my experiences. The privilege of my position in society, purely because of the circumstances of my birth, my gender, colour and race, had given me access to the world, but it had also limited my vision, confined my experience and sought to define my story too.

My story of Mother to this point had included the profound connections of biology and emotion with my birth mother. The deep pain when those cords needed separating and the endless changes that occurred and still manifest as age and circumstance evolve – joy, frustration, confusion, love and the suffocation that this love can bring, the sense of home and safety that abides deeply beneath it all. But my story had also begun to include a growing awareness of a sense of Mother within me, the yearning to nurture, the longing to give love, to hold, to create. Can I mother? What is Mother?

And so the picture of Mother widened, people began to come to me and share love stories that expressed deep longings for experiences of Mother and the feminine within their everyday lives. People yearning to be nurtured, to be loved, to be held. People began to express experiences of connecting with Mother and divinity within and beyond themselves. The call of the feminine; stories of Mother were longing to be told.

So here is a collection of stories about Mother. Stories of motherhood, of childhood, of longing to be a mother, of the inability to give birth, of the desire not to mother. Experiences of the feminine Mother rooted in all genders and orientations told to me by people from around the world. These stories weave narratives of nurturing and compassion, of love and connection, of loss and profound pain. Stories of hurt, resilience and beauty, of ecstasy and joy.

Gathered throughout the brooding spring of 2018 and into the furnace of summer, these stories are reflections and thoughts shared in a moment of openness, vulnerability and connection. They are not perfect: but they are perfect. They do not resolve, begin or end as fictional stories might. Each story responds to the emotions and experiences of the day we found ourselves in. They are hard and soft and brittle too. The stirrings of feelings, the outpourings of emotions long held, the stoic and effusive.

These stories gently and powerfully raise the voice of Mother, the narratives of the feminine. Narratives of nurturing and endurance forged through the lens of struggle, loss and profound emotion. They are the heart songs of people longing for freedom and acceptance. They are the tender murmurings of love and intimate connection. They are the wild and essential experiences of the enduring Mother, the compassionate feminine who, at her best, is rendered perfectly placed to help us re-member our communities into spaces of love and compassion.

Love and Presence

Since 2012 I have walked thousands of miles throughout the United Kingdom and I have spoken with people from around the world, asking them to share their experiences of love and connection. What are the loving narratives of their life? What does love mean to them?

Nowadays I find more and more people are asking me what I think love is. Having shared so many conversations, have I come to a fuller understanding of my own story? What is love to me?

I used to think that love was centred around people. Love was something of the heart that drew me to others and them to me. It was about a personal transcendent connection. It was something desirable, almost a perfection that was unattainable for me. It was about being wanted by someone and being needed by others. It was about not being alone.

But as this journey with A Human Love Story has grown, I have come to think that love is more about presence, about finding a place of stillness where I can allow myself to be. A space of presence where all the exterior noise can diminish and I can begin to connect with the essence of who I am. To honour my own being, to nurture my own journey, to love my own body and to hear my own voice. In that deep presence, I can also allow others to be – without the need to control them or judge them or shape who and what they are. A presence of being that allows a brave space to form where everything and everyone is welcome just as they are. Control and fear are diminished. In this allowing presence, I experience an expansive love.

Freedom comes into this experience too – freedom to just be, not defined by my experiences and my history, the places where I was born and the family that has shaped me. For me, love is a place where nothing of ourself has to be left behind or obscured. Every part of us is welcome and can be acknowledged. Love is a complete unveiling, a total acceptance.

And so the work of A Human Love Story seeks to create safe and brave spaces where people can meet and allow themselves to be heard and to be seen vulnerably and openly. In this presence, there is the opportunity for connection to grow. There is no judgement – only acknowledgement and open sharing. At their best, these spaces not only allow people to share their love stories but also to create new evolving experiences of love. In that space, all are welcome without reserve and without masks. All are heard. In this abiding presence, there is the opportunity to be loved and to love.

And so it has been with these stories of Mother. finding places of stillness and presence where I can meet with others and talk about how the loving narratives of Mother have shaped and continue to shape their lives. A loving interactive space where there is nothing but presence and time to hold and be held.

This is love as I experience it today, although I continually struggle to connect fully with all its implications. It connects me to myself, to others and to the cosmos. It is my emerging truth, dug from where I stand.

'Who is there in this world but Mother?
I am Mother, you are Mother,
Mother is mine, Mother is yours,
Everything is Mother'

Traditional Baul Song

1. I Was a Mother

Spring. Our last moments together. Sleeping in the garden, sharing memories, talking about motherhood, Shaman kissing your hand. And time. I held your hand a lot, I told you I loved you. I glanced at my feet, the grass and the bending trees as they moved in the endless breeze. Your hat slipped from your head and the sunlight engulfed your crown. There is no time.

·

You love your children in different ways. I feel complete when they are around, whole, safe. They have taught me to be affectionate, to be loving. We all needed to experience love in that way and they allowed me to be loving in that way. Motherhood is a selfless love, at least it tries to be, though it isn't always. It is something that abides in you, like instinct, like from the heart of you. I never wanted to work. I was a mother and they were my world.

2. Still Being Still

I find you in the car park, just as I imagined you might be: glamorously pulling at weeds. And we disappear deep into the ground of 'your place', where you take wing and fly, where you take refuge, moving quietly from room to room. And we settle in your working space either side of a large desk. You on your side, me on your side too.

.

Well, my mum had just had my brother. Within six weeks she was pregnant with me. And she was pregnant with me by someone else. So I'm sure she felt ashamed by the fact that, when she went back for her six-week check-up for her first baby, she was pregnant again. And so she didn't tell anyone. And she kept it a secret. I even heard that she went to Chicago for a while to keep it a secret. But she eventually came home. When she was in labour she told everyone she had a stomach ache, but in the end it hurt so bad that her mother took her to a hospital and there I was. So she kept me a secret and I knew that being in secret I had to be still. You can hear faster in water than you can through the air, and I believe babies can hear when people speak. And, usually, when people see women pregnant, they ask about them. You know, they're happy. You know, they ask, 'Oh you're having a baby, what are you having?' Well, I never heard those words – I was kept a secret, and so I stayed still. A few years ago, I noticed something. I had a canopy bed, and it was covered, and I loved it. And it brought back something: being safe inside, still being still. I remember as a child I used to play under the dining table and it had a tablecloth over it. I remember playing in closets. Not being put in a closet, but playing in closets and enjoying it! I like basements because they're dark, cool, covered.

And I think that's what happens while women are impregnated, while they are conceiving, while they are holding; whatever happens to them, happens to the child.

Once my mother had me, she now had two babies. We were just ten months apart. My mother was young – she was eighteen or nineteen. She was ready to move out of the house on her own and my grandfather said, 'You're not taking those children out of here.' So we end up with my grandparents, and she leaves and has more babies. So I grew up thinking, 'Well, my mum didn't want me from the beginning, right? And then she didn't want me because she left me with my grandparents.'

When my grandfather passed, I was seven, getting ready to turn eight, and my grandmother gave us back to our mother. When I went back to my mother, she had three other children. So I come from being two kids in the house to being five kids in the house, in smaller conditions. I had been eating chicken and rice for breakfast and now I'm eating grits for breakfast, and I'm eating cold cereal for breakfast, and baloney sandwiches. Well, it was a culture shock – it truly was and I didn't realise it. We wrote a letter and it went through the mail to my grandmother and it said our mother wasn't feeding us! Of course she was feeding us, but we weren't eating rabbit and rice every day.

When I was fifteen, my aunt said, 'You look just like your dad.' And I said, 'I don't look like James', and she said, 'Yeah, 'cause he's not your dad.' And I thought, 'What?' So, of course, I went to my mother about it. I'm fifteen now, right, and there's a big blow-up about it. And she said that my biological dad saw me when I was five but she told him that he would never know me and I would never know him. Later on, before she died, my mum told me to find my father. We didn't even know how to spell his name and I spelled it all kinds of ways and I could not find him. I knew the city where he lived. I was about to give up: I said 'Forget this!' and then something just popped up – his name, but the spelling was different. So I asked her how old he was and she told me and then I looked in this paper with the people's names, the address, the age and the telephone number. I looked at the age that was closest to his and I called it and it ended up being his sister-in-law – but he had passed. The story is he lived out of town while he was here with my mother. He was with her for a while but his wife came down and got him. So my mum was angry and upset and she never wanted to have anything to do with him. So I grew up believing that James was my biological father until I was fifteen.

At the age of fifteen, I probably was really upset and angry – mad, disturbed. Because then I had a child at sixteen. Part of the anger was, 'OK, I'll show you, I'll have my own thing. You didn't want me, you didn't want me to know my other people. So I'll have my own. I'll show you: this is how you treat a child.'

Later, I understood and I heard the story of my father. I heard that it was more of a love story that my mum had for my father. And it was the pain and the hurt that she received from him. First of all, she didn't know that he was married. And then, second of all, he left and never came back. Looking at it, that's abandonment issues, not trusting: those are things that I have today that I have to fight against.

And now, my youngest daughter just had a baby, six days ago! So it was Thursday morning last week that I was at the hospital and she didn't have the child until Friday morning. The pain was so horrific. She said, 'I don't know how to describe the pain but to say that it is painful. There's no words to describe it.' So at the end, at the very end, she was screaming, 'What is this thing? I want to see this thing that is bringing this much pain. What is this?' That's motherhood. That's what you will never, ever feel. That pain that comes with it. Because it is painful.

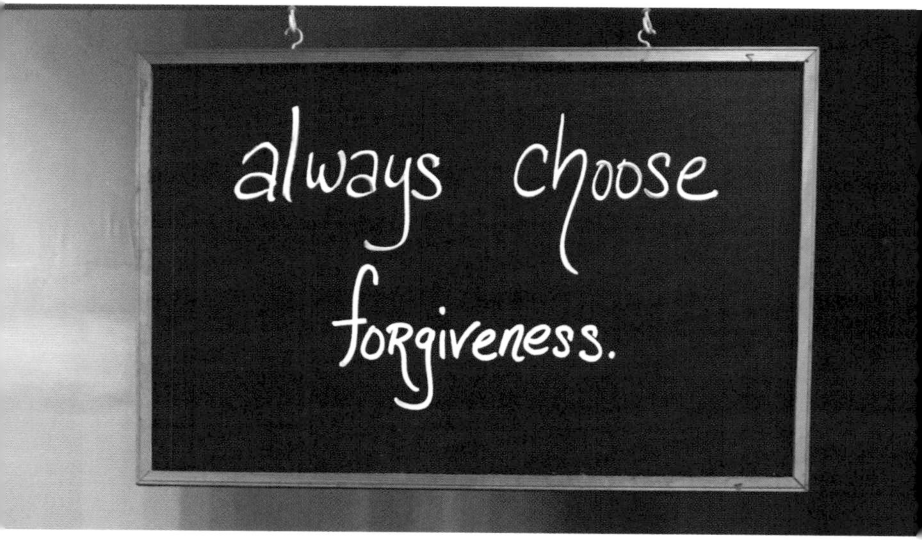
always choose
forgiveness.

3. They Come From You

I journey by car and already I miss the ambient grace of walking, the drifting into a place, the gentle movement through the world. I feel addled by this inhuman transition, the incessant noise, the discomfort; I feel removed from place somehow. But here I am amongst sofas and pillows and the soft warmth of your kind smile.

•

At the time when I met Jason's dad I was just nineteen and he was in the RAF. And we just had this attraction. I never looked at him and thought 'cwoar', but he was interesting: he was a bit different. I don't know what it was about it. He was thirteen years older than me. People say maybe he was a father figure. I don't know – was he? My relationship with my dad at that time had started to be a little more distant. You know, I was a teenager and I wanted to go out and do what I wanted to do, and they had less of a hold over me, I think. They had given up and said, 'Whatever, do what you want!'

I used to stay where he was quite a lot and be with him quite a lot and we kind of just got on with each other. It was easy. He came out of the RAF and moved to London so I continued to see him in London and he had jobs and did this and did that. I ended up falling pregnant when he was living in Lewisham, and it was a bit unexpected actually.

He just accepted the fact that I was pregnant and he accepted the fact that I would be doing the majority of looking after Jason (as he is now). And he kind of put that in my lap and sort of said, 'You know, really, Alexis, this is up to you. I know that it's our baby but this is your body. If you're going to have this baby you need to think very carefully.' But I wasn't overly upset at that. I was kind of grateful for the truth, I suppose. And I thought, 'Right, I need to come back home to my family then.' When I found out I was pregnant, I was kind of hoping we'd get married and live together. But from my point of view, he never really sorted it out. I wanted him to sort it out. I wanted him to sort it out, to get us somewhere to live and be a father and very much in our lives. And he backed off a little bit. Was it the responsibility, the enormity of it? I don't know.

There were times when Jason did struggle about his dad not being in his life. It came out occasionally – he'd get a bit upset because he was thinking his dad didn't love him. And it wasn't that his dad didn't love him. I don't believe his dad didn't love him. Not at all. I think that his dad doesn't know, perhaps, how to love – or to show love.

When I left, I was so upset and I was very emotional. I had this new baby in my hand. My sister came and collected me from the hospital. I know he was upset that I was leaving, but he wasn't providing me with anywhere to stay with our baby. I felt that, instead of doing something about it and actioning it, which was what I wanted him to do, he left it. So I thought, 'Right, I better sort this out myself then.' I always wanted him to make a stand for me and say, 'Come on, let's do this, let's get married. We haven't got any money but it doesn't matter.' But he didn't. I want Jason to know that I did love his father, but I wanted us to love each other romantically, and that probably was never going to happen. It was more of: we get on, we don't fight, so why not!

I remember having Jason and thinking to myself, 'At last, something I can do.' I kind of knew this was what I was supposed to be doing. I remember that. Such a strong feeling of my purpose of being a mother that it was really overwhelming. And then the importance of feeling that I was actually good at something. I could do this. I didn't need any qualifications – do you know what I mean? That I could look after Jason and do my very best for him. I knew I could do it, I knew that I could look after him and love him and this job was so important that I had to do it for the rest of my life. And it gets harder when they're older, actually. When they're little, you still have that element of control over them. As they get older and develop, all that changes.

The love that you feel when you have a child is the most amazing love – it's not like anything else that you ever experience, or that I will ever experience. Even though I love my husband, of course, it's totally different. They come from you, you made them, they're part of you. Everything from Jason is familiar – I just knew it. And the love that I feel for him: that's probably one of the scariest loves that I've got because it is so deep and it's different from the love I can put to one side.

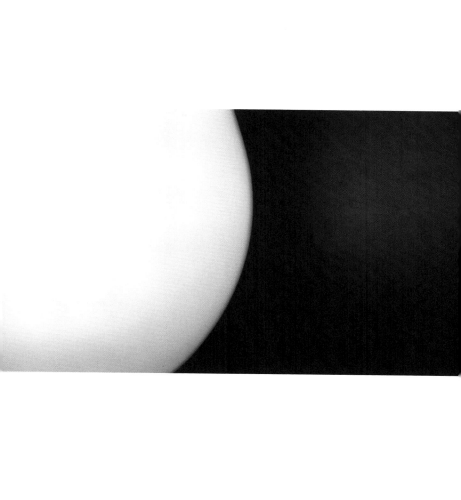

4. I Had to Tell Her It Was OK

Coffee, street, your mercurial look and silences that keep me uncertain. Then words that dart here and there, unfolding indirectly, weaving a patchwork of images and sounds. A poetic melancholy, an entrancing spell that journeys from Pakistan to England to home and beyond and onwards.

•

Theoretically, I've had two mothers in my life, as in my mother and my adoptive mother. But also I have two children, so I have known two other mothers as well, obviously now Ryoko, my wife, mothering my son. Which kind of excludes me sometimes. I feel like they're doing a better job without me, you know, because the relationship between a mother and a son is extra-ordinary. They don't really need the father sometimes. The father is there and, when he is called upon, he is expected to be there. But he's not needed all the time.

And that's really weird because I want to be there. I want to be the person he comes to – and I *am* the person he comes to –

sometimes he wants to be with me and he wants to sit next to me and he wants to hold my hand. But the mother is extra-ordinary because the mother is the one who gets his clothes ready and puts them in piles ready for the next day for his tennis or his school. It naturally comes, doesn't it? It just does.

I was adopted when I was six weeks old so I never actually met my birth mother. I went looking for her but I never met her. But I did read letters that she wrote to the Adoption Society. I went to Pakistan to try and find her but she had died seven years before I got there.

It was heart-breaking reading those letters. They're part of me, part of my history, part of who I am, I suppose. The only thing I've got from her is the letters and so they're powerful, very powerful.

There's a few re-occurring things in my life and one of them is what my mother went through and what she did. She came to England and she wasn't married and she was in Manchester alone. She was coming to England through the British Council to further her studies in education because she was headmistress of a girls' school in Pakistan. And she got pregnant out of marriage. The Council tried to help her and said, 'Look, if you are going to have the child then you can tell everyone in Pakistan that you are too ill to travel home, have the child and then go back to Pakistan, leaving the child here for adoption. No one will be any the wiser.' So that's what she did.

After giving birth to me, she went back to Pakistan but then decided she wanted to adopt me. But you can't just leave Pakistan. The law is still the same now: you can't just leave when you want to – you have to apply for a permit. And that all takes a long time. The court case was coming up about my adoption and she needed to be back in England in two weeks. So she was left in this situation that was impossible and she never made it back to adopt me. For her to be headmistress of a girls' school looking after children, having given up her child and being unable to adopt her child, it must have been heart-breaking. I never did get to say thank you in person, but I got to Pakistan to find out what happened to her. I did it, I wanted to do it, I needed to do it. I had to say to her that it was OK and thank her for going through what she did.

My adoptive mother is the most amazing woman and I never really understood why people said, 'Oh, you've got a great mother.' And I would say, 'Well, haven't you got a great mother?' She was just there, so I never really grew up thinking she was anything special. But in reality, now that we've all grown up, I can see that she is a great mother and she does great things for all of us. Being adopted by an English family – the only thing I think they ever gave me was love. And it always really annoyed me when adoption was brought up and the families weren't allowed to adopt a child unless they were of the same ethnic persuasion. I think they change the laws now and then – I think they go around in circles. If the parents are looking for a child and they want to give a child love, that's all it needs to be.

5. Being a Mother

I'm here in your home surrounded by books, tea cups and cooking implements. I can hear your footsteps coming down the stairs and feel the weight of all this stuff that is you and yet not quite you. And who are you? As we talk, I am profoundly aware of how little I know, how little I can share your experience, that pain, that love and uncertainty.

·

I do feel like a mother. And actually I think I felt like a mother before I was even a mother.

I always wanted children because I wanted a solid family of my own that I felt I'd never been able to have. It just didn't feel like I was part of my family as a kid. My mother was definitely not earthed. She had three breakdowns in my childhood. She'd had a hard time. She had my two brothers to two different dads. They had tumultuous relationships so I just grew up around a lot of anger and shouting and insecurity and violence.

On top of that was my mum's family, who were very high-pitched and highly strung and shouty. No one was solid. She was always there, but a lot of time she really wasn't able to be there. I've obviously always had an ideal of what a family should be. I just wanted square house, white picket fence, Mum and a dad, and a cat and a dog. And my mum just wasn't able to give me that. But that's what I always wanted and so I thought I'd create it for myself. In lots of ways, that's why I wanted to be a mother – and I feel like I have done that.

I guess it must work: two parents and some children? That must be a dynamic that works for some people. I just have never really seen it be, like, a well-functioning thing. It always just seems like hard work. Maybe I'm just too much of a perfectionist, or too intolerant? Maybe being on my own is easier? I mean, the kids drive me crazy, obviously, but I really like it when it's just me and them. I'm not always good at having relationships where I can just be myself. That may well be a lot to do with me as much as the other person. But, with the kids, it's not like that because they're part of me.

I had very different pregnancy experiences, even though they were only three years apart. The pregnancies were totally different, the births were completely different, their babyhoods were completely different. The experiences were just worlds apart.

I had only been with their father three months when I got pregnant with my first child. But it was on purpose. We knew what we were doing. We made a decision and did it. I was twenty-three and he was twenty-two. I was very young but, because I was very young, I had just the best pregnancy. I spent the summer just kicking about and sunbathing with my big pregnant belly, and it was fun. Giving birth was a difficult process. She was born by emergency caesarian in the end, but she was just the most perfect baby. Completely perfect! Just the biggest black eyes – perfect combination of both of us. I did think I was going to lose her whilst I was giving birth. I thought she was going to die and then, when I realised she wasn't going to die, I thought I was going to die. I truly believed I was going to die. It sounds quite dramatic now because I wasn't anywhere near dying, but I had just been cut in half and I didn't really know what was going on. I think it's partly a natural parent thing. It's the flip side of wanting to nurture something – that you really don't want to lose it. So you will imagine losing it so you can protect it. I think that's just how the human brain works, actually. You know the love that you feel for your child in your belly is unimaginable – it's not something you've ever experienced before. And so you do start to imagine losing it, because those things do happen.

The pregnancy with my second child felt wrong from the moment that I knew I was pregnant. Something felt very wrong – it didn't feel the same. I was just expecting a repeat of the first one, and it really wasn't. You know when you just sense that something is wrong and you feel uneasy and that uneasiness is throughout the whole of you? And then when I was six months pregnant, she stopped growing, stopped moving. And I could just feel the shape of the baby not moving in my belly and I had to give her a shove and move her around so I could feel a little wriggle and know she was alive, which was pretty terrifying.

And that went on for a month and, during that month, we discovered that there was a chromosomal abnormality, but they couldn't say exactly what. And then her not moving continued and she had to be born by emergency caesarean. And I can remember, in my mind's eye I can see, them wheeling her past me in her little cot and I looked at her and I thought 'she's got Down Syndrome'. I could just see in her face. And then they wheeled me into the recovery room. There were about seven people in there – doctors and nurses – and I was completely out of it because I'd just had an epidural, morphine. All these people standing over me and then they told me she had Down Syndrome, and all I could do was stare at the clock. And it was like something had split in my mind. Part of me went somewhere else. It was real traumatic disassociation. All I could do was look at the clock and wish that I was dead.

I didn't want a child with a disability. It wasn't my life's plan and I had no patience for any of that at the time. I was twenty-seven and just finishing my degree. We had thought 'let's have another baby, get it out the way so we can get on with the rest of our lives'.

I didn't go and see her for about two days. I just couldn't face it. I didn't love her; I didn't love her when she was born. And my mum actually gave me the best advice, and it was, 'Don't worry if you don't love her at the moment. Just behave like you do and it will come.' And it's true. I knew how to do the right things for someone you love and I just did those things and I developed a love for her. So it's a completely different love from what I had for my first child because I loved her from the moment she was conceived. I think the moment I really loved my second child was when she was in an oxygenated box with all sorts of wires in her and she wasn't responding to anyone, and I went over to say goodbye to her because she was going to go in the ambulance. She just lifted her little hand up to me and tapped it on the glass and opened her eyes. And that was when I knew. I always made sure I was there for every painful thing they did to her, for every injection. She had open heart-surgery when she was one, and I didn't need to be there because she was unconscious, but I just wanted to go through it with her – I just didn't want to miss any of it. It felt really important to witness that and to be there, to be that presence with her.

I still have moments when I think, 'I don't want to bloody do this, I really don't want to do it.' I don't want to have a child with a disability, and she does my head in. But in lots of ways I'm definitely a better person for having had her. It has been so stressful and I did have one moment of being sucked into a dark abyss and I was on the verge of losing my mind. It was a really scary experience. I have a really strong core. I've never lost the plot, and that has always been my biggest fear as well – losing it like my mum, because I've seen that and it is grim. I go close but I can't do it.

I definitely feel like a mother, and I definitely feel much more comfortable being a mother than being a daughter, and I've not reconciled that. I once said to my mum, it's quite a few years ago actually, that she was the first person to break my heart. And she really was, utterly broke my heart when I was a child. And I don't think I've forgiven her and I'm not sure how to. I think the more I love my kids and the more I give to them, the less tolerance I have for her. I just think, 'Do you know what, I haven't had it any easier than you: why couldn't you just do it?'

What's happening now is that my eldest is going away. She's getting to that point now where she's going to be growing up and going away. I've got four years, max. And it's amazing and I want her to be doing that but also the weird thing is I kind of feel a little bit relieved at the same time. OK, so it's happening, I know it's happening. I can feel it's starting but, at the same time, she's still such a baby. She wants to sleep in my bed. She's just dyed her hair black and she'll say, 'Oh look, we're like twins!' She still wants to be like me, so she's still a part of me.

6. To Be a Free Woman

High on the hills the wind blows hard and the shadows fall starkly on the gravel track. I wait for you in the lee of a copse. You are a friend, though we have barely met, but there is a sisterhood, a closeness that draws us tightly together. I am anxious, and a little giddy with expectation. I don't want to let you down but I feel my energy wilting and being swept up into the maelstrom. Sometimes I feel like this, like I don't have the strength to be here. Your voice rings through loud yet distant.

•

In childhood, I never really thought about whether I would be a mum or not. There would be other classmates where that would be so important to them; they were planning their weddings and they were thinking about baby names. Motherhood was just so central to them. But that wasn't the case for me.

So my parents divorced when I was two, and my mum was a single mum for a number of years. And then, in elementary school, she married my stepdad, who later adopted me. They had three kids so my siblings are eleven to sixteen years younger than I am. So it was like I had this chance to parent in some ways. I was kind of a third parent in the household and it gave me a really unique relationship to my siblings. And, as a child, I was probably given more responsibilities than I should have had at a young age. I was very independent. I loved the relationship I had with my siblings but I was also pretty burned out. I didn't need to parent anybody else – I was happy to get out and do my own thing.

When my partner and I got together, I said, 'I don't necessarily want to be a mum, so if you know for sure that you really want to parent, don't marry me; it's not a wise decision!' I think he was really pretending to himself that he wanted me more than to be a parent and it took him a few years to admit to himself that he hadn't really given up that hope. And so that was pretty stressful at that point because I felt like he lied to me, though not consciously.

Even before we were married or anything, I said, 'So if we were ever to have children in our lives would you be open to foster-care, adoption, or some other way of forming a family?' And he definitely was. And that question alone is a big shift and I'm continuing to realise how big it is. It's not just 'do we give a child a good home that's stable and all these things that we think we are?', because there is innately a hurt, an ache that comes from anybody who has been forming in one home, in the womb, and is then finding himself or herself in a different home. Whether it's at birth or six years old or twelve years old or whatever. There is this natural grasping for 'where did I come from and who are these people that gave me my genetic make-up?' And 'what's the story, what's the real story?' And then the deeper question is always 'was I unlovable?'

So my daughter Maya is seven and she is radiant, beautiful and a wise old soul and a crisp, just really powerful spirit. She's really strong.

Maya knows that her birth mum has three children in her care and that she is the only one that she had an adoption plan for. So I kind of feel this time coming in the future where one of her siblings, who's only seventeen months different in age, might ask Maya, 'Where did you get these opportunities from and how did you avoid some of what I've experienced?' And Maya will say, 'How did you get to be with Mum?' Some people say to me, 'You've been with her since birth so of course there's no trauma, she's just going to be raised like anyone else.' I say, 'Well, first of all, we welcomed her as parents but she did not get a choice and she still doesn't get a choice – because, when she's with both of us at the same time, she can't pretend that she doesn't have more than one family. Because she's multi-racial and we are white.'

There is a trauma for adoptees who are adopted at birth. Transitional times are hard and this has been a big transition time for kids in our neighbourhoods, in that they are getting out of school – and how do you make that shift? It doesn't seem like a big deal but then, for our child, those transitions are like a wave of abandonment, of, 'Wait, I had this teacher I loved and now what? What's gonna happen?' So, whenever we have these transitions, it shows up in our strong-spirited child and, instead of her always being able to name her fears, sometimes it comes out as aggression or anxiety.

I am standing in this place now of raising a multi-racial child and teaching her to know when to show others discipline and respect because it might mean her life some day, and also knowing that I am in this work of parenting to raise her as her fullest being: of being this strong, imaginative, creative, compassionate, reasoned, smart woman. And a free, a free woman.

And maybe that's the work that I am doing too. How do I be completely free knowing that the world doesn't know what to do with really free women a lot of the time? And then how do we figure out how to fit into the world we are currently in, in this time and place and setting? So, as I work on being a mother, I recognise that it's also the work that I'm doing for myself. How do I be strong and free in this time and place? And how do I not put too many layers on her of how the world might want to squelch her, but give her just enough? I can't protect her from racism. I can't protect her from sexism. But I can do my best to help her to be fully herself and know when it's safe to show up one hundred per cent or seventy-five per cent or when it's time to say, 'This isn't me but I'm showing up in the way that I have to for this moment just so I can live to the next moment.'

I love that motherhood is a responsibility and I have things to give but I also recognise my child's full humanity and how much her full humanness makes a difference to our whole family. Maybe the biggest surprise for me, as a mother, has been to recognise how often society treats children as less than full and complete beings. One of the wonderful things about parenting is that I see her as this full, human, important being and that we are becoming more fully our best selves together.

7. Be With Us

Early, too early perhaps, and our thoughts emerge slowly as if from a sunken ship. But in the simplicity of our connection you find clarity and truth. Even here and now. The morning chorus is carrying on outside and the busy calls of finches, blackbirds and wood pigeons drift softly through the open windows. Light penetrates every pore.

.

My grandma was very much the mother in many ways. She was the one who would sit with us and be with us and just spend time with us. That's what a mother is really, I think. They can just be there for you. Be with you.

She was a widow for thirty years so she mainly concentrated on us children and did what she could for us. She was always there, making something in the kitchen. At Christmas, she used to make all the puddings, and the cakes. It used to be a lovely smell when you came in – from the cooking. I shared a room with my grand-mother. She used to get very bad night cramps in her legs so I used to get up at night and rub her legs for her. It was nice.

My mother was in the factories. She was a welder and, in the war, she was a foreman of the factory. She was a real bundle of energy. five foot nothing and a bundle of energy. We used to go shopping together, and we spent a lot of time together. I do miss her. She was always so wise and said the right thing and gave the right advice because she was so level-headed. You miss that advice, even if it's on the end of the phone. She always said the right thing, and I'm terrible at making decisions. I can never make my mind up about anything whereas she could, straight-away.

I think when you lose your mother you lose part of yourself, really. And yet, in another way, you become stronger. You feel stronger because you have all of that in the background that you learned from her. I can't understand people who don't see their mothers, can't get on with their mothers. I think it's sad that they don't, because you can learn so much. Treasure your mother while you've got your mother, really. I think that's the best thing to do. Although you'll annoy each other at times, you'll miss them when they're not here.

8. I Could Feel Vulnerable in Love

We sit by the fire in the evening. Warm hospitality and gentleness. You both share as one corded together through the pain of experience. Outside, the wind blurs the sounds, and time seems to fluctuate. In the morning, you both walk me out along the paths north to the borders and leave me wandering onwards with your voices and memories still rolling around in my head amongst the silence of the hills. I want to cry, but no tears come.

•

S: My eldest son died about four years ago, four years tomorrow actually. It's the anniversary tomorrow. And we were in Australia when it happened. When the notice came through, Eddy was the one who got told to go to the police station to get some news, because my son was in America at the time. And Eddy had to come back and tell me that he had died, and I'd never seen him cry like that. From that moment and over the next few weeks and months, I didn't eat very much and I wasn't sleeping very well. And he completely took over functioning in every sense, getting us to America from Australia and dealing with everything that needed doing. And he completely took over everything and dealt with it and assumed that role and I just handed it over. He took over everything, even though he was grieving. He looked after and he cared for me and I'd never felt so vulnerable or as needy, and that's quite scary, because I don't think I've ever felt so vulnerable before. Needing someone in such a raw way and for him to be there and do it without any complaint. And, as the first couple of years passed, when I found it wasn't just about grieving, it was about dealing with not having joy in myself, and how to function for the rest of my life and me feeling quite low, he just quietly got on and looked after me but didn't make a big deal of it and didn't expect anything in return.

I think that's when I realised how much I love you and how much you love me, and that there could be a vulnerability in loving each other, rather than coming at it both with strength. And that's been a huge learning curve for me, to have such implicit trust, and it's made me love you even more.

E: For me, you were this kind of crumpled person. I so remember going to this Australian police station. And they came out and told me and I completely broke down. All I could think of was you and I thought, 'This is going to destroy her.' I remember saying to the policeman, 'God, why did it have to be Patrick, of all the people in the world?' I said, 'It's going to destroy her.' I said, 'I'd put myself in his place a hundred times.' I remember saying all this to the coppers and they must have thought I was mad. But I remember thinking, 'How is she ever going to get over this? How are we ever going to move forward from this point? It's just a complete disaster.' I suppose that is my love for you, because it was probably two, three years of you really struggling but I never thought, 'For frick's sake, I can't be with her any more', I just thought, 'Well, this is where we're at and I'm just going to be with you, just be with you. Do what I can and just be there for you.'

S: I think I never imagined I could feel love like that for someone who wasn't my child. I panicked a few times about whether you could still love me. It felt much like it was for any of the children. In fact, in some ways, almost greater because the need for you to love me and be there unconditionally was so strong. I needed it. I couldn't have functioned without it. And I think particularly with Patrick's death. He was my son but I had him when I was very young. I was seventeen and I was a single mother. So all my adult life, I'd been with Patrick – he was my one constant. From being a very silly, giddy little teenage girl doing too many drugs and drinking too much to suddenly realising and understanding a purpose in the world, which was love for this child. And then loss, but maybe then discovering my love for you. I mean, I knew it was there, without a shadow of a doubt, but it deepened or solidified from that implicit trust and faith in you.

E: 'Cause I didn't know you thought that really.

S: Didn't you?

E: Not like you've just said it. We just managed to do it, didn't we really.

S: We did, you did and you took me with you. I was committed to loving you but I never let myself feel vulnerable in that love. I always felt I could function completely well on my own because that was how I felt strong. So, to discover I could feel vulnerable in love and that it was safe was a huge learning lesson for me.

9. Letting Me Go

You usually seem so certain, so present. Though the season dissolves from spring to summer you hold firm, gentle and brutal in your unceasing presence. But today you sit before me uncovered; restless, you flutter like a butterfly, your vulnerability dancing before me in your words and laughter, as you cry and share your beautiful story. Gracefully you unravel and mend before me all at the same time.

•

I moved here when I was just turned eighteen. The first few years, I was exploring life and everything was great but, at some point, I felt this overwhelming sense of grief. And I couldn't understand what this grief was about. And I would just cry and cry and feel this lump in my throat and I couldn't breathe. And I kept asking myself, 'What is it that I am grieving? No one died, nothing happened – it's all OK.'

I live in this beautiful city by the sea and everything is so great. And then I felt it was somehow related to my mother, and maybe I really miss my mum? We have been living so far away from each other. It's a distance that I have created because, many times, I didn't call her or I didn't call back or I didn't connect. And, all of a sudden, after seven years of living here, I felt how much time I had lost with my mother. I was pursuing my thing, trying to know who I am, where I am going, really trying to know myself. And then there's this amazing person who was with me all this time and I completely cut her off.

I kind of put myself in my mother's shoes and thought what would it be like to have this baby and just be with that baby all the time, carry this baby for these eighteen years. And then this baby just goes and won't return calls. I mean, 'What the fuck?' So I really felt that pain of hers and I felt how strong she was not to bother me. She just had to sit with it. She knew I was going through something huge – a transformation of finding myself – and she never intervened. She just stayed where she was. I could feel how much effort that took.

And so, at that point, I started consciously making an effort to connect with her. And it was difficult coming back to really talking about things openly. I started making connections and talking to her about different stories and asking her about the things that I knew were important to her. We went through fighting until it all kind of collapsed together; how much I missed her, how much she missed me, and now I feel we're in such an open space. And now I'm starting to ask her about her mother. For the first time, I'm starting to ask her, 'What was her favourite song? What was she doing? What was she like?' And, each time, I can feel her grief opening, but she shares, and I feel like that's letting go.

After we started speaking to each other again I started to explore this grief further because I thought maybe this grief is not only to do with my mother. Maybe it's something more. So I started going deeper: 'What is this grief, how can it be mended, how can it be released?' So I went to a workshop where I was looking at really feeling my body and I felt this emotion rising again, this very intense grief. And I could feel there was my mother and there was her mother and so much history, so much history. All these mothers in line, one after another, passing down all of this history to me and to us through this cord, this umbilical cord, it's just all passed down. And, eventually, this line reached down to the earth and I could feel this ultimate mother earth and how much grief that mother earth held for her children, for us. It was the same kind of grief that my mum held for me and for her mother. Earth is the mother and we are her children and we are really like teenagers abusing, not listening, not re-connecting, not calling the earth. I cried for many days after that.

My father is a very Russian man, with everything that that brings. He is a very loving man but he just focuses on his work – nothing else, just work, work, work, work, work. And I understand why: because he felt that this was how he could really love us. And I feel his love and his effort and his commitment and also his pain and isolation. How much he worked, and how many times I was so ungrateful. The times were changing so much. I was born two years before the USSR collapsed, so they were changing times and he, like a rock, really held us.

But he was such an abusive man. He didn't know how to release his stress. So he would completely let it out on my mum and on me. Mostly on me and her – it never really reached my brother. After my brother left for university, he really lost it. Something really happened in him and it was a huge trigger. This is when the environment became so violent and so aggressive and my mum just held it, held everything. And so many times I thought, 'My God, why don't you just leave? Why don't we just go somewhere – surely anywhere is better than this?' But, first of all, she really loved him – she still does. And, second of all, she knew that no one would be able to provide for us better than him. But I could feel how alone she was.

He used to be very violent to us, and to me specifically. Later, when I re-evaluated everything and saw it from the side, it was not because he didn't love me but it was in his tissue memory on a cellular level – this imprint of, 'This is my right to abuse these women. They don't have the right to stand up or say anything.' But my question was always, 'Why?' I was a little kid. How could any father be violent to their daughter?

And, of course, there was a lot of guilt for leaving my mother – because we were a team, me and her. We would run away together. We would protect each other. She was protecting me, but I also felt like I was protecting her. The reason I left when I did was because she didn't need me any more. She was strong, really strong, and I feel like she had to learn a lesson of who she really is by herself without me or my brother. Not as a mother but just as a woman. Like, who is she and what does she really want and is that her ideal relationship, and if we don't need any more care from him, or support, then how could she live and love and expand? It was her chance to find out. I felt it was really brave of both of us – her letting me go and me going.

Things really changed in the last few years and I really felt the more work I did on myself, the more it changed. I feel like it's a better life now. When I go home now, we can be in the same room in a very different way. Definitely, there isn't any of the violence or any of the abuse – there can't be, as there isn't any space in my heart for that any more. So it's completely eliminated. My God, how different we used to be! There is so much emotion and so much pain and so much desperation but it is definitely coming from a place of more quiet and more still, saying, 'Let's not do this again, let's not do this ever again, let's see what's really important.' And what is important is our connection and our love.

And, as much as we go into the pain, on the other spectrum of that pain is this abundant unconditional love, because the reason why we experience so much pain, like with my dad or with my mum, is because we love each other so much. If I didn't love so much, I would just throw it away. But I didn't throw it away: he was in my heart every single day.

What really changed was when I really tried to put myself in his shoes. Sure, it was painful for me but I'm not the centre of the world, am I? There's also him and my mother and my brother. How do these people feel in this situation? When I really saw my dad for the first time, I couldn't have imagined. I thought he was this selfish bastard but he wasn't – he was just completely overridden by his own personal pain. Sure, women are so traumatised with so much grief and so many wounds but men are the same and maybe even more so. Because none of it is our true nature. Our true nature is completely one – it has no real gender. When I really connect with nature, it doesn't have a feminine or a masculine. It just is. Nature just is. Energy just is. It has none of the aspects of duality. So, for him and for us, there is so much pain because we want to stay in this duality.

I think it is changing now, though. The line is shifting. Look how much the world has changed in the last twenty years. And the ancestral pain is transmuting. We're purging, purging this pain.

That's why so much is coming to the surface. But the love is on the opposite side of the pain. As much pain as we have, this is how much love we have.

10. Little Beings

An empty chair, an empty kitchen. Just me and my recorder and a cup of tea staring through the window panes and beyond into the garden. Buddha sits immovable beneath the whispering trees. I can hear you moving through the house consoling, cajoling and gently easing your babe back to sleep. Silence falls on the house like a blanket. I hear your patient steps finding their way back to me.

Until I had my first child, I found that I was immersed in my job running my company. I was working six days a week, it was often stressful. And then, having a child allowed me to take time off work; it was an acceptable reason to have a career break. I found having children became the start of becoming more me. I felt work demanded a more masculine response to everything. Running a company, you have to be strong, you have to be a leader, you have to be resilient. There's little emotional capacity in that. The good sides of it are you get to create something you believe in, inspire a team and make your own decisions, but after building the company for fifteen years I really enjoyed doing the opposite.

Becoming a mother allowed me to leave those things to somebody else for a while.

I started off doing it to help my dad. I wanted to make a success of it with him. Work has always been very demanding, challenging and exhilarating, but I soon realised people had started to rely on me and that can be very pressurised. Whereas the family thing is just – it doesn't matter what the rest of the world think. You're providing for somebody but in a very straightforward, simple way. It demands a much more emotional response. Going back to work, I brought those things with me and created a better balance at work and home.

Being a mother gives me a sense of freedom. It encourages me to do the things that are for me, in terms of creative energy. You're raising little beings. You've got this complete love and trust circle going on, and everything you give to that child, you get back. You're building your own family life rather than just being a child or grown-up child in a family, you know!

When I had my first daughter, she just came along – she was our honeymoon baby, everything was easy, blissful. She was born at home in a birthing pool with my husband, my mum and the cat. No midwife. And then, when we went to have our second child, it was the opposite experience. So, from the moment we started thinking about having a second child, it felt like everything was difficult. Trying to get my body ready, trying to conceive, trying to hold on to the baby. I think we learned a new level of life – of how tough things can be. I remember going to see yoga people and they said, 'Well, you have to ask the universe, is there another child that is meant to come to you?' I was just,

'What? Is that an option?' I don't know if that was really an option in my world.

You know, that whole process really asked the question, 'Am I meant to be this mother again?' Through small highs and lows, to quite deep lows – losing pregnancies, thinking 'Was that a little life?' – I haven't found the answer. Different people have different theories, like babies come and go and just aren't meant to have a life on Earth. Or it is just the same baby trying to get down to Earth and eventually they make it when the time is right.

My losses were great and you have to go through it on a physical level, but my husband's loss was just as great and he didn't have the physical journey to help him process it. In a way, I think the physical journey helped me deal with the loss, because you go through a process and that helps you understand that things have come and gone. Some of my friends call me Warrior Mummy because of fighting for this baby.

I did finally get pregnant with my second child. I was in and out of hospital for the whole pregnancy. At times I wondered, 'Oh my God, is this actually going to happen?' I had to literally just lie on the sofa for nine months. And do you know what? He's really like that: he's super chilled and laid-back! It was like he was just trying to tell me, 'Do you know what, Mum, you just kinda need to make this really easy for me, and by the time I come into life you're going to have to take it a lot easier.' So I've learned a lot, and maybe that change had to happen for him to come.

11. Just the Love

Crowds upon crowds of people fill every corner of this overflowing city. All is noise, colour, water and movement. My ears burn, my eyes strain and my legs wilt a little as the rain falls steadily into every fold and crease of my being. Here in this deluge you find us, quiet and uncertain, with a story to share.

•

Today's my mum's eighty-sixth birthday and my family's going for a very posh afternoon tea. It's difficult to find a way of celebrating that really shows her what she means to me. It's an awful lot more than an afternoon tea! All my life, she's wanted to know as many tiny details about my life as I've been willing to share. She taught me to swim when I was in my thirties, because she was the only person that I would trust enough to save me. She would die for me. I've always known without a moment's doubt that she loves me. She has been there for me every step of the way. Every single step. And, amazingly, she has always understood me before I understood myself. What she doesn't understand is how great she is. She never has.

I remember playing with my dolls when I was very young and walking down the road with my doll in my toy pram. And I thought about how boring a game this was. But I also thought, 'I don't want to be a mother. I could never love anyone as much as Mum loves me and I wouldn't want to be less good at it than Mum.' That thought stayed with me from that day fifty years ago to this. And the feeling never changed. Not even when my brother and my close friends had children. I loved them but I had no feelings at all about wanting my own.

All my life, my biggest fear, of all my fears, was losing my mum.

In 2012, she got cancer. It was advanced. I fought for her survival with everything I had. I will never forget being in the room when she was told the news or the loving way my parents took it in together. I went into action, fighting to get her through it and having to be the one to break the news to my brother. Her chances weren't very good because her heart condition meant that she couldn't have the full chemo. I cried silently on the bus on the way home. It was very frightening, but I got through all those months of her illness with a single-minded determination not to let it win.

See how I talk about me getting through it! Me! I thought I had some kind of control. Ridiculous! But she did make it through, with great strength in her frail body.

Four years later, suddenly and without any warning, something very big changed in the depth of my feelings and understandings about life. As part of that, for the first time, I saw how selfish I can be, and how self-centred. I don't know who noticed but, inside, there was a massive change. And then, a few months later, my mum got ill again. For a while, I thought the cancer had come back. At one point, I thought that she had died. This time, through it all, even in the bleakest moments, I discovered that I felt and thought not about what it would be like for me to lose her, but about what it was like for her. I really *saw* her. I felt what it must be like to be her. It was an incredibly hard thing to do, but I accepted deep down that what mattered was the best thing for her, whatever that might be. Even if it meant something terrible for me.

Since her recovery, I've known that every day with my mum now is a gift. I wish I would find a way to spend more time with her. However much time I spend, it won't be enough. My gift to her is to love her now for the whole, wonderful woman that she is and not only because she's my support and an incredible mum. In her usual insightful way, she senses the change in me but I haven't explained it. It's too big and too deep for adequate words. Maybe it worries her. But it is a gift. It's incredibly special to feel what it is like to love her now without the blinding need. It's a big gift to her, not just to me. When she gets used to it, she will see that, for all of my life, whether she is here or not, I have just love for her. Just the love.

12. They're All Sunshine to Me

Early summer. On a ragged bench beneath the bluest of skies, beneath the swaying trees, we sit and talk. You hold within your frame a fragile power so intensely strong and yet temporal. A blur of passion and anger, of emotion and effusive energy. Mumma to many. A dog lurches across the field towards me and sniffs my leg before ambling away ambivalently.

.

The Milk Race was an old version of the Tour de France. It was an international cycling race. This was in the late '70s, so I was about eight. We went to see this cycling race, and Mum took myself and my brother. My brother was a couple of years older than me. We arrived there, and there were thousands of people. It was a huge, huge event. The roads were being controlled and we were all behind barriers. And I remember there were these international teams of about ten cyclists; an American team, teams from all different countries – and then there was a Russian team. And Mum made it quite clear to my brother that that was a different thing. And I was kind of aware from the telly, and that sketchy kind of awareness you have when you're aged eight, that Russians weren't seen favourably. In the press and the media and the news at the time it was 'Russia bad, America good', kind of thing. So I can remember being frightened when Mum said there were going to be Russians there. And then she said, 'But we're going to cheer them because no one else is going to cheer them.' And there was something about my mum that was so calm and she explained to myself and my brother that, 'It's not their fault what their government's doing. They've got nothing to do with it. They will have trained and worked as hard as all the other countries, and they deserve some recognition for that.'

Then the race started and there was a buzz in the background, and then the Americans came through and everyone cheered, and then the Russians starting coming and people actually started booing them. And I remember being really shocked and really upset. Perhaps it was my first experience of really empathising with another human being in their pain, but I remember feeling quite proud of the fact that we cheered and people did look at us really peculiarly. And it absolutely stayed with me in such a strong way, in a really conscious way.

When I started working with people in the criminal justice system, I literally knew from the first day that this was it. I knew there was no choice, because I knew in my absolute core that I could help them. And, because I could help them, I couldn't not help them.

And injustice just made me so angry. So many of the people that I've worked with over the years, either in the community, where I used to work with people after they'd been in custody, and now individuals in custody, have faced so much injustice in life and have experienced such distress and pain. It's palpable, and you can see it in their faces and in every disruptive, aggressive, unpleasant behaviour they exhibit. That's just their pain coming out. And I do have a sense that I am quite strongly in a maternal role at times. And that's not to say that it's all of my role, but it's a big part of it, because so much of what we need to do is re-parenting. We need to re-parent them because it went really badly wrong the first time in so many cases.

I used to work in the community with prison-leavers in a residential setting. Many of the men were massively socially isolated and felt a positive attachment to the residential environment where I worked, something they'd not experienced before.

There are a couple of men that used to come on public transport for an hour and a half every week after they'd left, just to come back for our weekly reading group. We weren't supposed to work with men that had left. They're supposed to move on. I used to get so frustrated being told, 'Oh, they're getting overly attached', and I would think, 'They've had nothing to be attached to for their whole life, and now they find something and we're supposed to take it away.'

I would read to them every week and do all sorts of nurturing things for them. I would bake for them every week. I would bake them a cake and bring it in and that, to them, was a massive deal – that somebody they saw as an official authority figure was giving up some of their private home time to do something for them.

I used to have men that had left back for Christmas as well, because I knew so many of them were on their own. And at Christmas you're really bloody aware of the fact that you're on your own. I would go in on Christmas Day and the men used to say, 'What are you doing here? You should be with your family!' And it was nothing, nothing. Time is the most precious thing, especially at times like Christmas. So, some have called me Mumma over the years.

We shouldn't have physical contact with the men. If somebody's distressed and in pain, it's incredibly difficult and feels inhumane not to reach out physically, even if it's just a touch on the arm, to connect and acknowledge that pain and distress. Sometimes men will try and embrace me, not in a planned way but in an instinctive way – but we're trained to say 'no' and step away from them.

When I've moved job locations, I've experienced the weirdest reverse-abandonment issues you can ever imagine. I feel like I've abandoned all those men I've been working with, and it's been really painful. And I feel – perhaps that's a real arrogance in me – I feel that no one else is going to look after them like I look after them. When I've moved, much to the amusement of everybody, I've spent significant amounts of time saying goodbye to every man that I knew I'd engaged with and had some connection with, because I didn't want to be yet another person who disappeared from their life.

And when I feel that something like that is important I'm dogged, and I've missed meetings and all sorts of important things because it was really important for me. And I worry about a lot of the men in my previous placements after I've gone. I've often had a strong sense of wanting to get in my car and drive back to see them, just to check they're OK.

So much of it is re-parenting. They're so un-boundaried: a lot of them have a complete sense of entitlement, and they have no confidence. The only way they know how to show their frustration with whatever is happening to them is through aggression, because that's worked effectively before. I call the men in custody 'Sunshine', because there's no way I can remember all of their names. Most of them really like it. They find it funny and laugh quite often when I say, 'You all right, Sunshine?' But I can tell they like it! You know, I spend my time with men who have committed the most heinous crimes – but they're all Sunshine to me.

13. Is It Divine to Feel Pain?

So many words and thoughts. The conversation flows and moves continuously from one tangent to another and, amongst all this beauty, we lean into divinity and love, anger and birth. But what do I know? I feel my self sinking deeper into the chair, hiding behind a pillow, quietly following where you lead as you let it go.

·

There's an assumption that loving your children is easy, the nurturing mothering thing comes naturally. There is also the assumption that, because all mothers give birth, that somehow childbirth is divine. I don't know! It's a traumatic thing. Even when it goes completely smoothly, it's so traumatic. And yet, it's just held up as this spiritual amazingness. I mean, I've never given birth, but the processes I went through were really traumatic. Really traumatic! And pretty much every single mother has either been cut open or ripped open. It's not easy just because we all do it. But I felt like, before I had my kids, no one spoke about that. No one spoke about it.

I felt guilty for years for having caesarians, and I felt like I had missed out on this amazing experience. I planned a completely natural water birth, no pain relief. What other thing do we go through in life where we say, 'Yeah, I'm just going to suffer this pain, I'm going to feel it because it's divine.' Is it only divine because it's happening to women? I don't know. Is it divine to feel pain, or is there a way of giving birth and having the greatness of that without suffering? And then, if it's a woman suffering, do we almost mythologise that and make it divine when actually it's just suffering and women are still dying in childbirth? For me, it's not taking it for what it truly is. Making it a divine experience silences conversation and shuts things down. Because if it is this amazing divine experience, you can't complain!

14. I Miss What Could Have Been

The earth is scorched dry. The silent weight of heat hangs over everything and the ground thrums in its thrall. Your tears fall openly and I can only watch and be alongside you and witness your story, share your experiences. Amidst all this latent heat there are no clouds – the sky is clear.

·

My mother was ill from when I can remember, so I don't remember any other way. We all loved her so much. She was around, she was very prominent and the whole of our childhood was centred around her and her care. But it was kind of unspoken really. We didn't talk about it. We didn't discuss it. It just was. It was our job. Our job was to look after our mum, which was lovely, and I loved her very, very much. That was my childhood, really: her being not well, and in different stages of that experience.

I always say to people that my life went backwards. So my life started with having loads of responsibility at a very young age; caring for her, feeding her, looking after her, trying to communicate with her. I think my primary role was the communication, because I was a bit smaller, a bit younger. It was my role to understand what she was saying and to get that across to everybody. She couldn't really talk but I could always understand, where the others sometimes couldn't, so that gave me a special bond with her, which was quite nice.

So we had a close relationship and, also, I was the youngest, so I still wanted some sort of mothering even though I was mothering her at the same time. It was a very strange relationship. It wasn't really like having a mother, in a way. You knew she loved you and you knew that you could sit close to her, but she couldn't really give you advice or protect you.

After being with us at home, she was in hospital for a year or two. When she came home for the weekend, she and my dad and I would drive down to the seafront and have a Strawberry Mivvi and doughnuts, if I was allowed them. Eventually, she was too ill, and there was a real decline and she was placed in a nursing home.

She died when I was sixteen. My dad didn't really tell us what was going to happen, so we weren't quite prepared for it. It was quite weird when she died, because her illness had been our lives, really. Not only had she died, but the whole of me in particular, the whole meaning of my life, was gone. I didn't know what my life was without her.

Up until she died, I was very sensible. I'd go out partying and be naughty and all that kind of thing as per usual, but I was a really sensible person. I wanted to be a social worker – this is what I wanted to be. I knew what I wanted! And then, as soon as she died, I didn't know what I was doing, I didn't know who

I was any more. And it took a long time, until now really, to rebuild again. I think that's why I never had children, to be honest – because I'd already had one, in a way. It sort of made me struggle to commit to people, I think. And I think it's only now that I've come to terms with everything and caught up with myself, because I lost myself for many years.

The whole of my life would have been different if we had just communicated and we'd been able to grieve properly together, and just been able to talk together. That's the bit I regret – that period of my life where I had some wild times but where I was very alone. And my friends became my family, as they do – but that's the bit I regret.

I could never feel: 'Why did you leave me?' I think it may have been helpful if I had. I couldn't feel bad feelings towards her. How can you be angry with someone when it wasn't their fault? It's just the way of the world, isn't it? It's so long ago and I can't even remember loads of stuff, but the pain is still there. It's not like I miss her, because I didn't really know her in that sense. I miss the warmth and all that kind of thing. I miss what it could have been. I think that's what I really miss. I miss having that key person who cares for me, and I've never been able to fill that gap – that's where I struggle.

15. I Want to Be a Mother

On 'the line' we talk and you are a thousand miles away and yet you seem even further from me somehow. I can hear your fragile words like whispers from another world. Here the eternal thrusting day pounds by outside the window: cars, dogs, humans, trade and talk, endless talk. There, all seems quiet. Just your shimmering words in a vacuum of experience.

•

One year ago I did think that I want to have a daughter. I would love to have a daughter. Sometimes, I think it's good, but when I'm too busy these thoughts disappear again. I think, in the future, I would love to have a family. Yes, I would love to have a family. I want to be a mother. Perhaps, sometimes when I think about it, I think maybe it's impossible, maybe I think that's where my emotion comes from. I like children a lot. I think now, because I'm thirty-seven years old, I am worrying that maybe after forty-five years old I cannot have children any more because of nature and the psychologies of my body.

And to have a child is not just a woman's thing – it needs a man as well! But right now, at this moment, if I really want to have a child, I perhaps don't need a man. It could be a donor. Maybe my emotion is coming from this question: can I have a child with a man or with a donor?

I didn't think about a family before but my dad and my mum are all very family-loved people. Really caring about their children, sometimes a bit too much. But I think that it's also the reason I think to have a family together is a good thing. I think, as a woman, I would love to have a family and children a lot.

16. My Little Love Affair

You tell me a hundred stories of love as we drink coffee. You show me how you disguise hemp milk in an almond milk packet so your daughter will drink it without protest. You cuddle your babe in your arms as he wriggles awake, feeds and sleeps again. You sit, immovable and certain.

.

The giving birth is something indescribable. It's so difficult to put that into words. And then to hold this precious little thing that I had been creating and growing and working towards for nine months – to finally meet him and hold him. The flood of love is just indescribable. And then our first night in hospital when it's just the two of us lying there. I barely slept, just wanting to look at him and sneak him into the bed and hold him.

And then, since he's been born, he's my little love affair in a funny little way. Maybe because of the particular energy coming out of him and the way we're connecting.

I want him to always feel safe, safe with me. My childhood

was quite challenging, with a rocky home life where the environment wasn't always safe, and I was scared at times and had too much responsibility too soon. I don't want him to have any fear of me whatsoever. I want him to always feel safe and know that he can come to me with absolutely anything and feel confident in that.

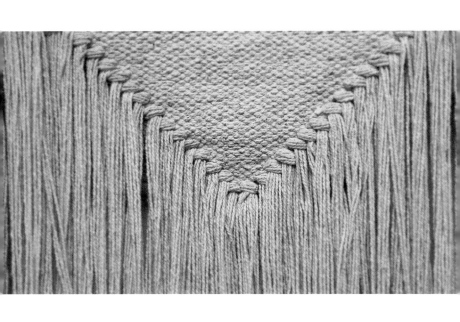

17. What Remained Was Love

The fields have turned from green to gold this high summer. The morning mists hang loosely on the shorelines and rising damp air fills the river valleys to the sea. The sun looms above the wavering horizon, bleaching the soils and dusts – claiming the day. And in this mounting furnace I remember your story, your voice, your glance. From Florida to Mumbai to here, where the white sun rages.

.

In November of 2008 my husband Alan and my thirteen-year-old daughter, Naomi, went off to India to be part of a meditation retreat, and they were staying at the Oberoi Hotel. This was a special trip for her. I was off in Florida at the time, visiting my family for Thanksgiving. And, in the course of that time, Mumbai was attacked by terrorists, who held the city under siege for about three days. And they had certain targets, and it turns out the Oberoi Hotel was one of their targets. As it turned out my husband and daughter were in the restaurant when the terrorists rounded the corner and shot everyone in sight. Everyone in the restaurant dove under the tables and the terrorists just went around killing them.

And all we knew back in Florida was that Mumbai was being attacked. And because we didn't know where they were and they were missing, my son posted their photos on CNN. And the website of the meditation group they were travelling with began to get emails from around the world sending love and prayers for them; for their safety. And then it was announced that they did not survive the attack and the emails came pouring in.

I was shattered. Life as I knew it was over. It was a numb state of shock. But what remained still alive was love. Love for my husband and daughter and for the family that I was with as we banded together in grief.

But then these messages started coming in from all over the world. From Muslims, Hindus, Jews, Christians – heartfelt messages of love. I didn't meet these people in person and I'll never know who they are. So-called strangers; because they saw those photos on TV and felt moved to sit down and write a note to me, sharing what they felt. And it was just so personal. We always hear about the one-world family and, in theory of course, we say, 'Yes, we're a one world family.' We would all agree with that, most of us. But to experience it directly is an amazing thing.

This was the big revelation of my life – that this world family became a reality to me. As much as my life had just ended, in the same moment my life was being reborn.

I'd like to read this to you. This is from the United States, Colorado, and she sent me a poem:

'With the salt of our tears and from the depths of our hearts a sea of love and compassion is born, so vast it covers the planet and fills all the worlds within it. As you search through the dark and lonely nights adrift on the waves of this enormity, know that you will be treated always by the rose dawn of love.'

And this next letter is from someone named Abed. It doesn't say which country. And the title is 'You are still alive'.

'Alan and Naomi, my dears. I didn't even know you and yet I love you. You are still alive inside our hearts and your peaceful smiles are still illuminating our world. Nothing can change this. I can't begin to think of what to say to ease your pain because I fear that nothing I can will. However, I have a feeling that your spouse and daughter are still near you – but looking down and smiling at you from a place more deserving of their gentleness and vibrant joy.'

This one is titled 'Let love live' – it doesn't say who it's from so I'll never know.

'We must all find a way to let love live. It's real and it has a basis in every living soul. Peace to all you kind souls in the world. Let's change the world, let's be kind to those who have hate. Only with loving compassion will we defeat the hate and the violence.'

Different messages. Over a thousand of them. This showed me who human beings really are, and what is at the core of our beings is love and compassion and a desire to reach out and connect beyond race, culture, beliefs, religions and all of that. So I became involved in a different kind of a love story: I started a romance with life, falling in love with humanity itself. And that's what has been my survival and healing, because I still feel it. The loss is still there. It doesn't go away, but you learn to live with it and then just shift the focus. It does keep the love alive – it keeps them alive.

I have learned that the first gift from life is love and the last gift my daughter and husband left me was love. It is not from ashes to ashes, dust to dust. It is from love to love and whatever happens in between is up to us. I cannot let this love die along with my husband and daughter. I can choose to rest in the arms of love in any moment. I can keep my heart open with acceptance and appreciation for all that life brings. How can I be more loving in the face of any challenge? I will always come back to this question for the rest of my life.

18. I Was So Young

The burning sun of the solstice is losing its heat and the cooling night softens the edges, allowing me space to think and breathe. Here, in your garden, we talk. The sky falls backwards, stretching time as we sink into our chairs and into the gentle murmur of the coming darkness. I am in awe of your humble sharing, your brave narrative and the constancy of your compassion. Before us, the wheat fields sway their choral consent as the sun sinks low.

•

I was so young, so young when I married, I was just a child. I can remember the first year of my marriage was so hard, because I'd never been away from my family. I couldn't imagine my kids getting married at that sort of age now! When you're together at such a young age, you modify your behaviour, I think, to make that relationship work – and it's the same when you become a mum. I just kind of assumed that's what you did, really. I'm not career-driven, but I loved what I was doing and I kind of had a path that I felt I was going to follow, and I never thought having children would change that. I just adapted my life to encompass that new reality. When I had my first baby, it was just the next step.

I'm eternally grateful that I had my children very young, because I had several miscarriages and I couldn't have any more kids after that. Also, I could never have foreseen that my marriage was going to end. For quite a long time of my marriage, I probably was quite controlled – and that's a terrible thing to say because I'm a really strong, empowered woman. I think, when you're a young person, patterns of behaviour evolve without you realising it. Because of the nature of my career and the personality that I am – I'm a nurturer and a carer and a giver – I would always try and make situations right. So, if there was a financial problem, it was easy for me to go out and do an extra couple of nights. So, without realising it, I evolved into a person that I'm probably not. I lost 'me'.

When you're constantly told it's your fault, or you're not attractive, or you're not the person that you think you are, you do tend to lose your confidence. I suspected for a long time that he was having lots of affairs, so that was really difficult – really difficult because when I challenged it I then felt very bad about challenging it. And I was also very alone, because I didn't tell anybody about it. I think that came from being very young. I felt I'd failed because, on the surface, it looked like we had a beautiful marriage and beautiful children, which we did have – but, actually, the person underneath was not a beautiful person. It was really hard to tell people that my life was actually really different, and I'm not the strong person that you think I am.

Suddenly, I was a single mum at such a vital time in my kids' lives, and the person I thought I was married to was not that person at all. So, in a sense, my whole life had been a lie. And, financially, I imagined, after being married for so long, that we would be a little bit protected, but I was literally left with nothing.

We were on a family holiday, and that's when it all came to an end. Unbeknown to me my husband chose to fly back to England without telling us. It was such a horrendous time and it has had a major impact on my life. As a mother I chose to stay on the holiday surrounded by loved ones, but it was a very traumatic time. When we returned to England my husband had removed everything from the house and we never really saw him again. I suddenly found myself in complete shock and in a position where I did not even know where to start.

As a mum, you want to protect your children so much, with that motherly instinct that you have. And the hardest thing for me was that their father didn't have that motherly instinct that I had. It didn't matter if I had nothing, as long as I was with my children. But the disappointment that he wasn't fighting for them was so hard to reconcile. Because, if it had been me, as a mother, every single day of my life I would have been fighting, and I'd still be fighting until the day I died to see my kids, to apologise, to do something. For me, the biggest disappointment was that someone could walk away from their children and never see them again.

For them, I think it must have been so hard, because not only had they lost their dad, they kind of lost their mum too, because I was never that same person again. But, also, I was trying to make everything perfect – and you can't make everything perfect. I think I was trying to be this perfect mum. I tried to shield them from everything. I was allowing them to be angry and hurt and cross – it was a lot to carry.

I did three jobs, and I got my son and daughter through college and I paid their rent. I'd go and do a day job and then I'd work in the evening. There are times when I think, 'Wow, it's a big responsibility to be a mum and a dad', because it's just me. It's just me, with that overwhelming feeling that you still have to make everything right. I never actually really stop, and I don't know why that is. I think, when you're a single parent, you constantly challenge yourself the whole time – 'Could I have done it this way, should I have done it that way?' So, I don't ever feel safe, and that's a terrible thing to say.

I'm a very different person now, and surrounded by really amazing people, which I think you have to have in your life. And I have two amazing, beautiful children that have done so amazingly well. You know, they're so grounded and I have to sometimes remind myself of that. I think we did really well.

It's hard now as a mother when you get to this stage, because my life is not how I imagined it was going to be. Where do you go from here, really? Sometimes, these paths are meant to be, aren't they? And I am eternally grateful that I had my beautiful children and that I am able to follow a different path now. I feel it's incredible that we've been able to come through it all, and I feel blessed every day that I've been able to experience that.

19. A Way of Being

You enter the room a bundle of energy sitting immediately next to me, comfortably greeting me. We talk, and the talk goes deeply inwards and outwards. We cry a little, share some truths and explore our yearnings of the heart. We arrange to meet the next day, and so it seems to go with us. Thank you for your courage and welcome – until the next time!

·

You asked about Mother – and I was thinking about the yearning of our world right now to embrace the mother figure as a way of being in a place of seeing and hearing one another, and being at more peace with one another.

And that this yearning is on a bigger level than just how we do motherhood: these human, mostly biological relationships. In this bigger sense, what is being called out is 'how we can welcome and give more power to the divine woman, the divine feminine, within each of us'. With all the pressure and strain we're experiencing as individuals nowadays, it's no wonder that we've got the call to return to this nurturing, mothering female energy within all the spheres of our life and our political life.

There are examples of very successful matriarchal societies throughout our human history, and even today. And there are ways of infusing our daily lives and our political lives in ways that honour the more feminine within all of us, not just women. The qualities of nurturing, compassion, of intuition, creativity and presence. And we are aching for that now. Our communities need that now. So this does seem to be the time.

This isn't just about motherhood or mothering on a one-on-one basis, but how we practise society.

20. Thank You

We move between the pages of your opening heart, the transforming, effervescent and evolving core of your being. Lavender bushes, screeching traffic, a chocolate bar and a distant car alarm hold us – the day is coming to an end and the first pangs of autumn hang in the air, the next frontier emerging as the light deepens.

●

We've always been so close. I'd say she's got amazing tough love within her. She knows me so well, and I know her. She's good at unconditional love and being tough when it's needed. She's been there through thick and thin with me. I mean times when I've been through quite dark episodes, and she's helped me through that. I think she's a very practical person – she knows what she wants. If she has something in mind, she will achieve it. Nothing will get in her way or, if things do come up, she'll always try and find a way of overcoming things, and that's been quite inspirational to me. I think, without my mum's love, her unconditionality and acceptance, it might have gone a different way. It is in my nature to be naive and trusting of other people because that's down to a condition I've got, which is autism – high-functioning autism – but she's given me tools through which I can grow.

I live at home with my mum. There have been talks about moving out. Actually, when I was younger, I was extremely resistant to that – I never wanted to leave my mum. Ever! But now I do want to move out, and I feel ready for it. There have been plans talked about and I did have a plan of moving back up north as a possible option. I fell in love with a location there called Redcar Beach.

Having the courage to let your child be independent and free, when all you probably want for them is to be near, is a part of being a mum I suppose. I always thought, if I moved up north, I would hurt Mum's feelings. But there has come a point now, when I say 'I am ready to move out', that I can add 'I would like to move out now' too. I've got my mum's best interests at heart as well, and I feel that I can't stay in this same place any more. I think that maybe this moving up north thing is an enhanced external expression of what I'm feeling inside.

I'll always love my mum, but I cannot always be with her. In letting me go, it must be like she's birthing me out again. Being taken away from the womb again and the pain happens again but, this time, it's an emotional pain and not a physical pain. Maybe that's what we'll both feel. And maybe all children feel that and all mothers feel that too.

I mean, I'll always have my mother in me because I'm her child. I'm her daughter. It's like waves, the ebbs and flows. It's the same, though it's different at every moment. Through every transition you go through. If I could say something to her I'd say,

'Thank you for giving me this once in a lifetime, quite literally, experience!' She is physically – and on all levels – the author of my creation and I'm so happy and proud to be her daughter, and I'll be her only daughter like she'll be my only biological mum. If I become half the mum that she was to me, then I consider that an achievement.

21. This Is As It Is

Amongst children, girlfriend, dogs, pencils, cups and activity, we talk our way into your experience. A myriad of sounds fill the room and my recorder crackles with overload – the red light flickering agitation in my peripheral vision. I am overwhelmed and moved by this full world of interaction and exchange. Colours, sounds and smells engulf my lethargic body – I am moving into love, becoming lost in the moment, in your togetherness and your intricate connections. I leave late, hopeful – the energy swiftly ebbs from me and I begin a lingering journey onwards.

•

I've been a mother for a long time, because I had my first child at seventeen. I didn't feel that I was missing out but I suppose, as time went on, as I got to my late twenties and my early thirties, I started to feel that I wanted to explore the world and explore who I was as an individual more. And I started to go out more and I started to experience life more and I found that it became quite difficult to actually juggle motherhood and be that individual person. What is it that I actually want to do with my life, and how can I match that into being a mother? What is it that I want for them? What is it that I want to show them?

More and more over the years, and I would say especially in the last four or five years, my role as a mother and how I view motherhood has completely changed. And I think that's to do with my yoga practice, meditation, working more in holistic care and really discovering who I am as a person. And I've realised the greatest gift I can give my children is me living my truth. It takes a lot of self-healing. From the things that my children say to me, they know that I've been through struggles. They know that, before I found yoga, I was not looking after myself very well. I hit a breaking point in my life, in my early thirties, and they were caught up in that mess. But, in going on this healing journey, it's actually helped heal them, too, and the respect that we have for each other now is completely different. The teachings that I bring into the home they are really receptive to and really inspired by.

I know as a mother that I've done that letting go, and it's the biggest gift that I've done for them. And it has had profound effects and really helped me to see that holding on to them and not letting go of that attachment is like drawing them into my world, my mess if you like. It's like a cord and I could really see that clearly. I was drawing them into my attachment, like a dependency almost. It's like, if you don't let go, you're not giving them full permission to step into their own power.

I run retreats. I'm running one in Bali and my daughter is going to be coming with me. And, of course, I'm looking after a group of people and I'm a little bit concerned. It's an opportunity for me to juggle my work and motherhood and not really see it as two separate things – but to see it as 'this is what I do', this is my life, and my daughter fits into that.

And there's part of me that's really nervous and already trying to control the situation and also let go as well: like telling my daughter, 'You can't speak to me like that in front of people – you know that, don't you?' And you can't do this – and do that! I'm trying to control the situation before we've even gone there. But this is real. This is as it is. Why am I trying to hide my motherhood from my work? Why would I do that? So it's trying to let go and allow things to naturally occur through that process without being fully in control.

When I hit that difficult point in my early thirties, I wanted my life to be very separate – and I did deliberately try to do that: this is one life and, when I come into motherhood, this is my other life. The two were very separate, and there would have been absolutely no way that I would have involved my children in my other life then – because, one, it wasn't suitable and, two, because it was mine. It was mine and I saw it as my individual self. But it was destroying me. It was a life that was destroying me, and I was trying to hide that from them and so it almost had to be separate, because I wasn't living my truth and I didn't want them to see that. So I put on masks and I was able to juggle very, very well, actually. I would say I was probably the master of juggling! I was very good at putting on different masks in different situations that I needed to be in: one for friends, one for work, one for motherhood, one for when I was going out. And they were all very different and each group of friends would tell me how amazing I was in each different mask. So I got commended for motherhood, I got commended for the work I was doing at the time. I got commended for when I was out with my friends and being the life and soul of the party. So all these masks were serving me in that stage of my life but, deep down in my core, it was slowly crushing me. It was very difficult to keep all of that up.

But I don't need to do that any more; I don't need to keep separating myself. I don't have any different masks any more. It's a process you have to go through, I think, to come into that fullness of who you are.

22. We Are Not Everyone

By the river the day moves effortlessly by. Crowds of tourists chatter as they make their way to the theatre, strolling along the riverside in the late summer sunshine. We meet and talk beneath a willow tree by the water's edge. I don't know how we came to this point beneath this tree, on this day. Though we have never met, you share your story vulnerably, and with such strength too. A swan takes to the water, turning courteously before gliding away on the current.

•

Even before my eldest son was born, it was just violence all the way. He would go out drinking, partying till one and two in the morning. It was just constant beatings. We had a penthouse built for us because of his job and, when he came home I could tell by the sound of his feet on the floor what mood he was in. He would come up in the lift, open the roof door, he would walk over the roof and open our door and then his big bunch of keys that he carried around with him would get thrown. And I knew then that that was it.

Or he would say, 'I'll be home by six,' so I'd have his dinner ready. He'd come in at twelve o'clock or whatever and say 'Where's my dinner?' So I would say, 'Well, it's no good now. It's still in the oven but it's no good.' Or he'd pop in for half an hour to have something to eat – I'd bring the dinner in to him and he'd say, 'I'm not eating that' and that would go up in the air. Sometimes, he would come in from the pub and he would sit in the corner chair. I'd be on the settee, shaking. And he would glance over every now and again, smirking at me. And he could keep that up for as much as three hours – the mental torture. And then, eventually, he would say, 'Get your clothes off,' which I wouldn't do to start with because I was a strong character but, because of the kids, I didn't want to scream or cry, you know! I mean they'd seen quite a lot and they'd heard quite a lot, but not everything. So he would often start hitting me and sometimes he would hit me until I was on the floor, kicking me and stuff. That's how I lost one of my ovaries – with kickings.

Funnily enough, I was thinking the other day, 'I bet when I die and they examine my bones, they'll be full of fractures,' because I never, ever went to hospital. I had black eyes, busted mouth, I lost all my teeth. I didn't lose them straight away but over the years I lost them. And for a woman to lose her teeth, it's so devastating. It changes your face. Your confidence is completely gone, you're frightened to talk to anybody. I couldn't go out for weeks and weeks and weeks.

We left many times but, on this occasion, we ended up in the Battered Wife's Refuge. We got there at eleven o'clock at night and there were three women that opened the door and let us in. There were a dozen kids there screaming, fighting. They were literally climbing the walls. So our first night there, we shared with this woman, her fifteen-year-old son and a couple of other kids. They put two little beds up – one for my two boys and one for me and my daughter.

Now, earlier in the week, one of the kids' teachers had given me a little card. She used to pop down and see me sometimes because she knew what was happening, and I can't remember what was on it but I just stuck it in my bag. Because, when you're hurting like that, you don't want to reach out to anyone, because there's a lot of shame attached to it. So I had just stuck this card in my bag. So, anyway, I thought I'd just sleep in the chair at the Refuge for the rest of the night. I had my eyes closed and started to doze off and, suddenly, my daughter screamed and the fifteen-year-old boy was trying to molest her. So I ended up, literally, sitting in front of my daughter so she could have a sleep to keep this boy away. So, eventually, at about six o'clock in the morning I thought, 'I'm taking my kids back. I didn't bring my kids up to live like this. I'll take whatever comes. If he kills me, he'll kill me, but I'm going to look after the kids. I'm taking them back to their own little room.' So I sat there for a while and then something made me open my bag and look in, and I put my hand in and I pulled this little card out. And, whatever was written in that card, in that moment I read it, it was like someone had come in, given me an injection, and I was filled with this kind of power. And I thought 'No', and I kissed the card and I put it in my bag and I thought, 'We're going to get through this.'

Because, being a mother is, in itself, powerful. When you have children, you develop some kind of power because you become their protector. You become their teacher. And you just love. The love is there for your kids. You may not always like them but the love is there. For me, it's all about quality time. You could spend a year with your kids lying in the grass and have no connection. So it's the quality time you have. And, as you're giving out to your kids, it sounds weird, but just to have your kids sitting there and looking at you and really listening – that's like a power in itself. It comes back to you. Love is the feeling that comes from bonding through giving your child your all. One is not born to love – it comes from a series of events and depends on the type of character you are. And, when faced with adversity, it's the love for your children and their love for you that makes you determined to protect them while trying to maintain normality.

They were there for some of the beatings and my eldest boy, quite a few times, would faint if I was hit in front of him. My daughter was the little fighter – she would grab his leg and my youngest boy would be trying to grab hold of his other leg. I couldn't stand that my kids were having to try and protect me, and that's why you scream silently, because not only do you not want your kids to see, but I wouldn't be able to bear my kids screaming, because that's what would happen. So you try and do it quietly. Sometimes you can't – it's so hurtful, you can't.

We ended up eventually in Queen's Park in London in a maisonette. No furniture, no nothing. And Mum gave ten pounds out of her pension money and I went out and bought one big piece of cheap net to cover the windows, a little pack of elastic and a safety pin. I threaded it through ready but we had no screws or anything so we went round feeling all the walls, seeing if we could find a couple of nails and we did. And then I took my high heels off and I stood on my eldest's shoulder and I used my high heel to bang the nails in. That's how we started our new life together. But it was the happiest time in my life because we were so free. Oh my God, we were happy, and I think we were there for about two months before I found how to turn the heating on. It was winter time and we were frozen, but it was Home.

We lived six floors up, and outside at the end there was a chute that you could put your rubbish down. And everyone used to take their big black rubbish bags and, instead of emptying them down the chute, they would just leave them underneath. And it really used to annoy me: 'Why can't they just send it down the hole?' So, one day, I said to my eldest son, 'Take that bag down and put it in the chute.' So he came back and I said, 'Did you do the rubbish?' and he said, 'Yeah.' And I said, 'Did you put it down the chute?' And he said, 'No, Mum, it's piled up with black bags down there so I just threw our bag on top.' So I said, 'Oh, did you? Come with me!' And I made him go down and climb up the pile of bags, fetch our bag and then put our bag of rubbish down the chute. And he was fuming, and my other kids were laughing, saying, 'That's really stupid, Mum!' I said, 'Listen to me. We're not everyone. We are not everyone. We've got dignity. We've got no money. We've got nothing. But we've got each other and we have dignity. Never forget that.' That's the strength. That's what keeps us strong as well – holding on to that dignity. I used to say to my partner, 'You can break my body but you'll never break my spirit', and he never did. Emotionally, yeah, and physically too, but there was always something strong inside me. You don't lose who you are. Do you know what I mean? You just disappear for a while.

23. Spiritual Mother

In the blacks of night beneath a half moon we sit. The fire crackles and the smoke engulfs us in this tiny cabin. Surrounded by pots, Marmite jars, matches and hats, we wait. A deep peace descends and the fire brings us into a gentle abiding, a comfortable sharing that is so human that we barely need to speak. My earthen feet hold me to the floor and the wheels of my mind still in the trembling silence. Somewhere in the distance Britney sings out one more chorus, the goddess dancing before her people one more time; and then silence, and you and me and the fire.

·

I love my mother so completely. She was such a perfect being for me as a small child growing up. She was this perfect constant companion who was always there, and always kind and always loving and always wise and patient and intelligent and talented and funny. Great fun – so joyful. She was just the best thing – she was divine and is divine and we do have a divine connection.

When I was going through my young adult years I often wished that, if I could just be more like her then I would be OK. Then I would have done something in the world worth doing. But I wasn't really like that. As a woman, I was very masculine and very out of balance and very lost. I was also brought up in the '80s, where it was far more fashionable to be male in this capitalist time. So it has taken me a while to find my feminine, although it was always there. So when I became an adult, I wasn't always interested in being a mother.

But my mother was my best friend and, as I got older, I longed to re-create that relationship. And I longed to be a mother. And I got married, thinking that my marriage would be for that, but it just wasn't, and isn't. I'm just learning to accept that my life is different than my wants and desires, and growing my child in my own womb is not my calling. It's been painful. I still feel some grief, but I've come to terms with it.

My teacher says that one of the best things you can do for the world right now is not have a child, because humanity is in crisis in this time of great change and this time of human evolution. And I've always known that I never really wanted to put a child through that.

When I came to the point in my life when I'd stopped trying to have a child, and I'd accepted that I wasn't going to have my own, grown from my own womb, I went to see one of my own students give a talk. The first time I met this girl she came to me and she was like a tiny sparrow with broken wings with no song and no joy. And I went to see her give a talk, and she stood on the stage and she shone and she had wings the size of an eagle and she just soared, and she was so beautiful and eloquent and powerful. And I looked to her and it re-affirmed to me that I do have children in the world and I will have many children and not just one or two.

I am a mother. I've always been a mother. I've been a mother to the tiny broad bean I grew as a little child, because I could always feel and see the life in everything. And I am a mother. I was born a mother with this deep nurturing and this deep love of the Earth and all things in it. But a mother is also brutal and powerful, like the Earth, and like a lioness with her cubs. She has also this cutting, brutal strength you have to have to be a mother. Of protection for your young and for yourself. So, as I've got older, my vision and my experience of Mother has become far more complex than I could have imagined and I really surrender to that, which gives me great peace.

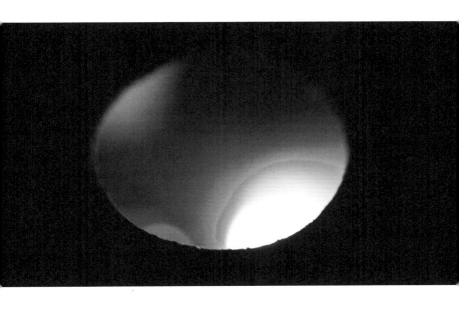

24. Fierce Love

You make me feel nervous and curious and out of place somehow. Maybe it's my age or the personification of your youth and powerful vibrance. Today, you seem calm and relaxed, almost sleepy, and I hear the autumnal murmurs of a yawn down the crackling, stuttering WhatsApp line. You in your place, me in mine, both looking beyond.

.

Throughout my life, I have always understood Mother through the lens of my own birth mother and then my grandmothers, and I'm thinking particularly of my dad's mum, who was very timid.

I feel that, for so long, I associated Mother energy with Mother Mary energy and this timid, pure, meek and mild Mary that we are told about in a lot of Christian faith and theology. And I associated my dad's mum with this same meek and mild kind of mothering. And then, later on in my life, some of my earliest formations of Mother were through the Yoruba spirit tradition of Cuba and the spirits of that tradition – and one being, Yemaya, the Great Mother. And then I felt I tapped more into this power, this oceanic power of love, and the unconditional love of the great Mother and just how powerful that is; how powerful and queenly it is.

And then, most recently, I think I'm coming into this understanding of Mother Mary and all that she embodies. Now, it really feels to me that the 'meek and mild' is really inaccurate and really just a strategy of Patriarchy to make feminine power look meek and mild. But there's so much fierceness in Mary's example, just like that fierce love and fierce commitment to one's path and the fierce commitment to spirit. And just the power, the immense power and the immense love and compassion.

Nowadays, Earth, for sure, is the biggest way that I experience Mother – just tuning in to the infinite and eternal love and the deep immanence of that loving presence, that all is deeply here and available. She feels like my mother so fully, so much. I feel so much devotion to her, to the divine mother, and I understand the divine mother in so many ways, but one of the ways is definitely through Earth herself.

Sometimes, in my loving, I feel that deep capacity to hold and to love and nurture in relationships and in life and that feels motherly to me. But maybe it feels a little bit more like lover energy than Mother energy. And I think this might be just age – that Mother isn't something I feel super, super called to, or that I've had deep experiences with. And, in terms of my own mothering, I don't know if that will be a life path that I will choose. I mean, it very well could happen, but it's not on my radar right now. I don't know how my life will unfold.

your life unfolds in proportion to your courage.

25. *A* Mum – *The* Mum

Such a gentle morning today. So calm and clear. I can hear the sea whispering to me in the distance and I feel at home here, maybe for the first time. The light is spectral about me and everything seems in its own time. There is no rush, I am here. And, in this great calm, we meet. The sea rolls on, the light holds. I feel so grateful, so in love.

What is a mother? Before I was fostering, you were called a 'foster mother', but then that term was changed, because a lot of children had their own mothers but their families had broken down and they were being removed from their mother and father and siblings and were being given homes with strangers. So then you became 'foster carers'. And the emphasis in language changed the roles slightly – but, actually, what we were still doing was giving care, and the continuity and the support and the love unconditionally to young people who hadn't had it or who had lost it or had been denied it in their life. For all the change of words, the role was still a 'foster mother'.

What you did, and still do, was to provide something different: a warmer, safer, kinder world than these children have come from, where they have suffered all different kinds of abuse. So you come into their lives and try to deal with all their anger and their rage. They've given up with adults, you know. They've given up. So you're in a position to say, 'OK, but this is my home and you're welcome and you can just be here and make your mistakes with us.'

I fostered about six or seven young people over about six years, because I had people for a whole year, mostly before they moved on to more adult lives. So it was teenagers at their quite tough stage. One of the problems with fostering is that children get moved a lot – so they stop forming attachments. They cut off to protect themselves. Things break down, and they break down much quicker than in a traditional family set-up.

Usually, if you've got your own children, you hold onto them through their storms – but these children can be so stormy that it's hard to hold onto them. With one young man, I was up at the custody centre practically every week. The police were round every week, and I held onto him for one year before he moved on. But it was that sense of giving continuity. We always said that every day is new. Every day, we start again. Whatever is happening, you just start again.

I don't know what a mother feels like, because I've never had a birth child – so I don't know what a birth mother feels like. My mother was very possessive and would say, 'All I ever wanted was my children around me. I never wanted you to go away. I never wanted you to travel.' And I felt very oppressed. The thing was, my father was a free nature. So I had the two models. I had the free nature father with his unconditional love, and my mother with the unconditional love. But, within the conditions that would make her feel better. So I chose to model myself on my father more than my mother. My mum was really funny and lovely, but she just had her own problems going on and didn't know how to let go. My aunt used to say to her, 'You really have got to let go of your fledglings, your little birds.' So the relationship with my mum was complex.

What put me off being a mother was seeing my sister go through a very traumatic time being pregnant and being kind of forced to go into marriage and have a child, and always being quite bitter and regretting it. And also seeing how it impacted our family. My sister's generation were the generation before the pill, so a lot of girls got pregnant quite young. It was the '60s and all the older sisters were getting pregnant. They were really poor – they had no money, and had gone through totally traumatic break-ups with young boys who were in their twenties. And quite a few of my generation watched this and didn't have children. They didn't see any of the support systems in place. It was a really difficult time for me, so the first thing I did was go off to Africa as soon as I could after art college – just get out of the whole family crisis. Family for me meant crisis. I was twenty-eight when I set off for Africa and it was the best thing I ever did in my life. 'My eyes didn't blink,' I said. For a year, my eyes didn't blink. That's what it felt like.

I went through a period in my forties when I would go into Mothercare shops and just want to buy stuff. In my late thirties, when a couple of relationships had not worked and I was by myself and things seemed really tough, I just wanted to have kids, but I was always afraid to have kids without a partner who was really stable. I think the fear was being really poor. Fear held me back from being a single parent and I think that was a shame. But, then, when I was teaching, this young man came along who'd lost his birth mother when his brother was born. Emotionally, his father cut off from them and then he was in this terrible civil war in the Congo. And he landed in my class. He was about sixteen or seventeen at the time and a self-elected mute, practically. He wouldn't speak. You could just touch him on his shoulder and he would jump through the roof. He was suffering from terrible post traumatic stress disorder. He'd been nearly killed in the forest. He was left for dead, tied up on a tree. The marks are still all over his body but, luckily, the soldiers were too drunk to realise he wasn't dead, and he was rescued. He'd come from a wealthy family and so got to another country, and was then flown out to England.

After a few years, his friends started to say to me, 'Ah, you're his mum', because I'd helped him. When he was in hospital, I'd got people to visit him and just gone round to see him now and then because he was so vulnerable. Then he was homeless, so I had a little flat and he and his friend rented it from me. And I heard him saying to people that I was his 'mum', so I said, 'All right then, I'll adopt you' – he was about eighteen then. And it just gradually developed and flowed. This is over twenty years ago now. We just kept contact and then, when his little boy was born, he would say, 'This is your grandson', and so it just eased itself into my consciousness, having been a bit of a joke before. But, clearly, he needed a parent to help him in a foreign country. And sometimes I'm Jo and sometimes I'm Ma. It just depends.

Yes, I do feel like *the* Mum, but I don't know if I feel like *a* Mum. I feel like *the* Mum – but *a* Mum? I wonder if anyone can ever, really – if they haven't been through it – deeply understand what childbirth is. I think it's something that grips your body and your soul and your mind, and it's something I know I haven't experienced. So the physical and unconscious linking of giving birth and your body taking total control of you as you birth another being — I haven't had that experience. This is for me the '*a* Mum'. But I've had the experience of nurturing, being there — good or bad — come what may, still there, constant. A constant little star in the sky every night: still there, you know, whether the storms are crossing it, whether you're not even looking at it, it's still there. And I feel that, maybe, *the* Mother is what I can be to people and to young people. And, maybe, the constant star is a symbol of what *the* Mother is — the symbolic recognition of someone who's always there, whatever crisis hits, who's able to support someone through the extraordinary journeys of life, who's a few steps in front in the timeframe but has got some experience to pass on, some lessons to help you on a conscious and unconscious level.

And love. You're giving an example of love, and unconditional love. I think that's what it is: *a* Mother goes through, for me, the physicality, the body changing and the natural birthing. But *the* Mother is the representation of what we hope is the best that a child, a young person, anybody, can receive love and wisdom through. So it's to do with love and wisdom, isn't it?

Epilogue

A few days before handing in the final draft of this beautiful collection of love stories I was invited to participate in a Havan, an ancient fire ritual in the Vedic tradition. So along with many others I gathered in the early hours of a wild summer morning and found myself immersed in a living, moving offering. The fire danced in a pit in the centre of our gathering and we shared prayers and blessings in song and chant. Ghee, flowers, nuts, fruit, rice and incense were offered to the fire, blessing this elemental energy and representing our personal sacrifices: the burning away of our old selves for renewal and purification in body and mind.

And, as this ancient ritual continued, we made blessings for Father and Mother, Shiva and Shakti, incanting one hundred and eight names of Father and one hundred and eight names of Mother before the fire. And, as each name of Mother was recited, I began to see you, my friends who shared your stories here in this book. I saw your faces, your motherhoods, your births, pains, your joys and your loves, as you were swept up into this dance, into the flames of this essential experience. I saw mothers, daughters, the feminine in all forms and the Earth herself: all nurturers, carers, intuitives, creating and bringing forth life. And it all danced in the flames before me like a dream: the empathy and compassion of the Mother, the female liberated in all genders and orientations, finding its creative healing power taking root in all spheres of culture and community. It was a compassionate encircling embrace and I cried for the beauty of that deep expression.

And, above all of this, the last stars were disappearing into the morning sky – the cosmological dance of life and death fading away before the dawning light. This dark Universal Womb wherein the stars and planets are born and die before us every night. And does not the whole of the universe and all of space encompass the Mother? The womb of nurturing wherein life is given and brought into existence.

And the traditional song of the Baul echoes in my head:

'Who is there in this world but Mother?
I am Mother, you are Mother,
Mother is mine, Mother is yours,
Everything is Mother.'

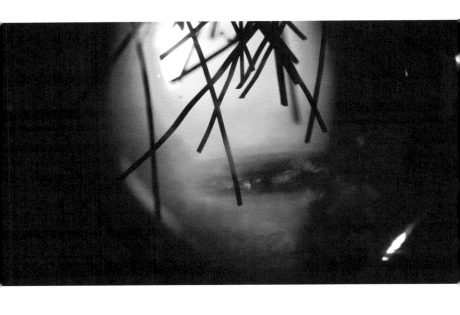

Mitákuye Oyás'in

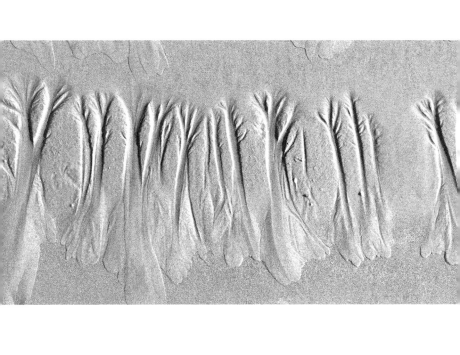

Footnote

I have never felt so humbled as when sharing these stories of love. As I have journeyed into these conversations of the heart, I have found myself awakening to a more expansive expression of Mother. Through these experiences, I am beginning to feel that motherhood and Mother are less about what we are, the physical function of giving birth, our biology, and more about how we action ourselves in this living experience. And if Mother is rooted in action and not just biology, then it becomes a transformational space where all genders and orientations can find a mutual home and expression. Mother, at its best, is nurturing, loving, constant, intuitive, fierce and creative, a gift of compassion available to us all, from us all. Mother is transcendent, not fixed to physiology, gender, orientation, colour, race or nationality. There is no division. As biological mothers, creatures are impelled to physically put themselves aside to give birth to their young. As *the* Mother, each of us has an opportunity to choose to set ourselves aside for others and inhabit the world as a nurturer, a carer, an intuitive, a healer. In this way, I am Mother and you are Mother, and we can all help constellate a more compassionate world rooted in love.

Acknowledgements

As with all endeavours of the heart, the inspiration, mechanics and the creative force was shared. Particularly so when the source of the inspiration is the heart stories of others. The stories are the book and so each author who opened themselves out to share deserves all my gratitude and love. Their capacity to explore their humanity, and gift that exploration to others within these pages, is grace itself. Thank you.

Once again, the bright guidance and insight of those folk at Birlinn Publishing must take equal credit. The nurturing wisdom and incisive editorial eye of my dear friend and champion Ann, the thoughtful consideration and support of Andrew, my editor Helen Bleck, Jim, Debs and the entire team have made this book available to you in such a beautifully conscious way. Thank you.

Love and gratitude to Miranda Sawyer for her connection, thoughtfulness and words of introduction to this book. Respect to Andrew Nim for his inspiration and friendship.

And so to my family. As these pages took form, we all went through the physical loss of our mother, grandmother, great-grandmother and friend respectively. We wept and drew together and reshaped our family experience in the light of her stellar absence. I love you all and I am so blessed to have you in my life.

Grandma, these pages are for you – born in a different world and subject to the whims of that world, you burned brightly and bravely and stayed with us for so long. I love you and I am forever grateful. And Mum, Mother, who nurtured me into this world and carries the weight of my existence every day – thank you for bringing me forth. Thank you for your bravery and enduring love. I love you.

And, finally, to Petra, my love. You are the bravest person I know. Thank you for being you unflinchingly, for loving where others can't, for nurturing the life in others where I fail. I love you completely.

And I think these pages must especially go out to my beautiful nieces and nephews, who each hold that compassionate powerful spark of femininity within them – joyous, raucous, creative, loving, sensitive beings growing up in a world where the future can seem uncertain. Cherry, Fraisie, Harper, Jake and Harry: blessings on your journey – you are so loved.

Share Your Story

Anyone, whoever you are, however you feel, and in whatever place you find yourself, can have the opportunity to share your story and be heard. Write, phone, email, invite me to come and share. Become part of this evolving journey of connection and love.

If any of the sharings in this book have raised any strong emotions within you or you wish to share your own thoughts and feelings, then there are some wonderful people local to you who are there to help you and allow you space to process your feelings. Don't be alone – the greatest healing comes through connection, through allowing yourself the opportunity to be heard and allowing someone else the opportunity to listen. Visit my website to find further information and some links to places where you can find connection: www.ahumanlovestory.com.

It is a courageous act to be vulnerable, to truly give and share. But what a gift to yourself and others! A gift of connection that allows us to transcend and expand the consciousness of our waking experience and to glimpse our shared divinity.

Matt Hopwood
Email: matt@ahumanlovestory.com